To:

Keep writing. You are awesome and inspiring!

God Bless

Sierra Leone Joyce

5/31/17

Black Man I Choose You

Copyright © 2006 by Roland Ashby Rier

All rights reserved. No part of this book shall be reproduced or transmitted in any form or by any means, electronic, mechanical, magnetic, photographic including photocopying, recording or by any information storage and retrieval system, without prior written permission of the publisher. No patent liability is assumed with respect to the use of the information contained herein. Although every precaution has been taken in the preparation of this book, the publisher and author assume no responsibility for errors or omissions. Neither is any liability assumed for damages resulting from the use of the information contained herein.

This is a work of fiction. Names, characters, places, and incidents either are the product of the author's imagination or are used fictitiously. Any resemblance to actual events or locales or persons, living or dead, is entirely coincidental.

ISBN 0-7414-3138-6

Published by:

INFINITY
PUBLISHING.COM

1094 New DeHaven Street, Suite 100
West Conshohocken, PA 19428-2713
Info@buybooksontheweb.com
www.buybooksontheweb.com
Toll-free (877) BUY BOOK
Local Phone (610) 941-9999
Fax (610) 941-9959

Printed in the United States of America

Printed on Recycled Paper

Published May 2006

Table of Contents

A Note From the Editor	iv-v
Dedications	vi-ix
A List of Poems and Poets	x-xii
Lover	1
Love	1
Morning	2
Him	2
Black Men I Choose you	3
Don't That Black Man Just Make You Wanna Scream?!!	4
If I were a Billionaire	5-6
Cut From the Same Cloth	7
Spectator of Love	8-9
Have I Told You Lately That I Love You	9-11
Arrogance	12
Colors	12
Untitled	12
Untitled	13
You Thought of Me	13

John 3:16	14
Dear Daughter One	15
Dear Daughter Two	16
Dear Daughter Three	16
Dear Daughter Four	16
Untitled	17
Love	18
Black Child	19
Rope	19
Rags	20
Khadijah	20
A Daddy Hoped For	21
Momma's Here	22-24
July, 1967	24
April (A Dedication)	24-25
It Wasn't Supposed to Happen, But it Did	25-28
Time	28
Heaven	28-29
Home Sweet Home	29
Pride	29
I'm Different	30-31
Pursuit	31-32
He Told Me What I Wanted To Hear	32-33
The Heart of a Mirror	33-35
From the Heart of a Fat Lady	35-37
My Christmas Evolution	38-41
Crystal Ball	42-46
Nikki	47
Sdia	47-48

Mom	48-49
Debbie (1959-1979)	49-50
Lord	51
God Is	51
Mary Magdalene	52
A Change of Rules	52-54
I am My Momma's Child	55
Biography	56-59
About the Editor	60-61

Notes From the Editor

The Black Man has been chosen for many events in history. Some of the following are:

- For Slavery
- To design the city of Washington, DC. Benjamin Banneker
- To liberate the Black Man from racism in the United States and in the World. Dr. Martin Luther King
- To fight an historical battle in the Civil War
- To be one of the most outstanding or the best fullback in the National Football League, Jim Brown
- To write about a mythical character in literature "John Henry" the steel driving man.

The Black Man has demonstrated that he has charisma, motivation, determination, and a will to bounce back until success is achieved.

The father of Tiger Woods was not a touring pro on the Professional Golf Association; however, he turned his son into a touring professional pro on the PGA.

The father of Venus and Serena Williams was not a touring pro, but produced daughters who became a fixture in time and space in tennis. "A Black Man doesn't have to be a pro to train a Pro." (*Ms. Beatrice Carter*) *

*Ms. Beatrice Carter is an outstanding English Teacher at Ballou Senior High School, Washington, D.C. In addition, she is an outstanding Amateur Tennis Player

As you absorb these emotions, the feelings of these poets will engulf you in a universal feeling of love.

This editor has chosen the following Blacks who invented items that have household names, and some are forgotten. They are:

- The Lawn Sprinkler, J.W. Smith
- The Pencil Sharpener, John Love
- The Lawnmower, John Burr
- The Elevator, Alexander Miles
- The Mop, Thomas W. Stewart
- The Typewriter, Lee Burridge
- The Golf Tee, Dr. George Grant
- The Dust Mop, L.P. Ray
- Gas Mask
  Traffic Signal, Garnett Morgan
- Seed Planter, Henry Blair
- Early Spark Plug, Edmond Berger
- Telegraphy, Granville T. Wood
- 300 Uses for the peanut
  100 uses for the soybean, pecans, and the sweet potatoes,
  George Washington Carver

Dr. Roland Ashby-Rier, Editor

Dedication

Portia Y. Bookhart

- To my "Dad" for being there always for me and providing a safe, nurturing environment, for showing me that you can "be," just believe it.

- To my "Mom" for being in my life and for loving me.

- To my sister, April, for being that peace of heaven.

- To my sister, Cheryl, for trying and succeeding in life on her own terms.

- To my brother, Robert, who has brightened my life immensely.

- To my cousin, Khadijah, for showing me "there is a way."

- To my nieces and nephews, life is what you make out of it, make it the best.

- To the best friend a girl could have, Sam.

Dedication

Dianne A. Carson

- To my mom, Ruth, whose relentless perseverance and undying independence taught me to endure regardless of circumstances.

- To my Godmother, Sister Way, who taught me to love God and not try to understand.

- To my sister, Debbie, who taught me to be nurturing amd kind.

- To my daughter, Natalie, that helps me to walk a straight and narrow path.

- To my grandbaby, Lindscy, who is the joy of my life and makes life worth living.

- To my best friend, Jackie, who sees only the good in me and believes that I can achieve anything.

- To my best friend, Stephanie, who believes that I am the best and always tells me the truth.

- To my best friend, Brenda, who always seems to draw out my strengths.

- To my loving departed friend, Darryl, who taught me to live life to the fullest.

Dedication

Sierra Leone Joyce

- To my dearly, much loved, departed parents, it was only through God/s infinite wisdom, that I was blessed enough to be crowned with the distinct title of "daughter". I hope that you are happy in the life here after as you were before.

- To the brother that left me, I will miss you always.

- To Cheryl and Godfrey, I will love you always.

- To daughters, Tifanne and Leander, keep your chin up, head to the sky. The glass is always half filled. Dreams do come true.

A List of Poems and Poets

Love

Name of Poem	Author	Page
Lover	Dr. Bookhart	1
Love	Dr. Bookhart	1
Morning	Ms. Joyce	2
Him	Ms. Joyce	2
Black Men I Choose You	Dr. Bookhart	3
Don't that Black Man Just Make you Wanna Scream?!!	Ms. Joyce	4
If I Were a Billionaire	Ms. Joyce	5-6
Cut From the same Cloth	Ms. Carson	7
Spectator of Love	Dr. Bookhart	8-9
Have I Told You Lately	Ms. Carson	9-11

Tidbits of Wisdom

Arrogance	Ms. Joyce	12
Colors	Ms. Joyce	12
Untitled	Ms. Joyce	12
Untitled	Ms. Joyce	13
You Thought of Me	Ms. Carson	13
John 3:16	Dr. Bookhart	14
Dear Daughter One	Ms. Joyce	15
Dear Daughter Two	Ms. Joyce	16

Dear Daughter Three	Ms. Joyce	16
Dear Daughter Four	Ms. Joyce	16
Untitled	Dr. Bookhart	17
Love	Dr. Bookhart	18
Black Child	Dr. Bookhart	19

Childhood

Rope	Dr. Bookhart	19
Rags	Dr. Bookhart	20
Khadijah	Dr. Bookhart	20
A Daddy Hoped For	Ms. Carson	21
Momma's Here	Dr. Bookhart	22-24
July 1967	Dr. Bookhart	24
April (A Dedication)	Dr. Bookhart	24-25
It wasn't Supposed to Happen, But It Did	Ms. Carson	25-28

Life

Time	Ms. Joyce	28
Heaven	Dr. Bookhart	28-29
Home Sweet Home	Dr. Bookhart	29
Pride	Ms. Carson	29
I'm Different	Ms. Carson	30-31
Pursuit	Dr. Bookhart	31-32
He told me what I Wanted to Hear	Ms. Carson	32-33
The Heart of a Mirror	Ms. Carson	33-35

From The Heart of a		
Fat Lady	Ms. Carson	35-38
My Christmas	Ms. Carson	38-41
Evolution	Ms. Carson	39-43
Crystal Ball	Dr. Bookhart	42-46

Death

Nikki	Ms. Joyce	47
Sdia	Ms. Carson	47-48
Mom	Ms. Carson	48-49
Debbie	Dr. Bookhart	49-50

Inspiration

Lord	Ms. Joyce	51
God Is	Ms. Carson	51
Mary Magdalene	Dr. Bookhart	52
A Change of Rules	Ms. Carson	52-54
I am My Momma's Child	Ms. Joyce	55

Lover

I'm longing for my lover
But he is not here
Away, far 500 miles
Oh, how lonely I am
I'm longing for my lover
But he has not called
I don't dare imagine
That he didn't have a dime
Or didn't have the decency
To tell me… it's over.

Love

Love is so fragile
So delicate
That you have
To take special
Care of it
To keep it.

Morning

I always wanna smile
When I wake up
With you in my bed
In the morning

Wanna smile and shout
From every mountain top
How much I wish
For morning
To find us again
And again, and again

Him

His smile, soft and dangerous
Could split the Red Sea---
There was music in
The silence between us;
His cologne was calling
Sensuously in my head and
Then
He was gone
But the laughter will last
A lifetime

Stars sing songs when
Time knows no hour---
Mystery in the power
Of all that is new
Night, Oh Night
Oh, don't be late
For morning will not wait

Black Men I Choose You

Black Men, I choose you,
Because you are beautiful
Beautiful minds, beautiful bodies
And souls to match.

Black Men, I choose you
Because you are great
Great writers, great orators
Great lovers, friends, and teachers,

Black Men, I choose you
Because you are cerebral.

Black Men, I choose you
Because you are strong
Black Men, I choose you
Because you are creators,
And together, we can create
A black world.
Black Men, I choose you!

Don't That Black Man Just Make You Wanna Scream?!!

Oh, how that Black man
Just makes me wanna scream

Like how he can see right
Through me
And tell me what I'm thinking
When I still don't quite
Know myself

Like how he can keep me
Up all night
Looking for the answer
When there isn't one

Thick –
Like a tree
Dark
As a secret
Rich
As the soil
Able
As a mighty river

Oh, there's just something
About that Black man
That just makes me
Wanna scream!

If I Were A Billionaire

Billionaires are people
Who can make love
To that special someone
At 2:00 AM in the morning
Or at 2:00 PM in the afternoon

Billionaires are people
Who do not have to depend
On blankets to keep warm-
They can spend Christmas Eve
Listening to Christmas carols
And have the where withal
To know how priceless
Companionship is,
Especially during the holidays.

Billionaires are people
Who rush home from
The airport
Because someone special

Awaits
Their long and
Overdue return.

Billionaires are people
Who have eyes that dance
When they look at
Their mate
And have long since
Graduated from the
Solo-ism of life.
Billionaires are people
Who can finish each other's thoughts
while speaking

Billionaires are people
Who truly know that
Even when the gas tank
And the checkbook
Are on E,
Their real wealth lies
In one another.

Cut From the Same Cloth

Red, Yellow, White or Black
Could have any color man I want, but I want a
black Man
Some say, the blacker the berry, the sweeter the
juice
I say the berry ain't sweet lest it's a black berry

He looks just like me
Hurt the same place where I hurt
We came over on the same ship
Bled from the same beaten whip
Separated, belittled, scorned
We have a history

He know what I mean when I talk 'bout Martin
Luther King and Malcolm X
My tears mix with his when they call him "boy"
and I know he is my "Man"
'Cause we cut from the same cloth
Sewed by the same stitch
You can't pull us apart
We mesh together from the heart

Red, Yellow, White or Black
Could have any color man I want, but I want a
black Man
And I ain't shame
We have a history

Spectator of Love

On the coldest day of October
On my way to a Shakespearean class
She, in a worn raincoat with shoulder length white hair
Was using a cane for assistance.

He, in a tattered jacket, silver gray hair, and spectacles,
Was wearing an old cap.

Unaware that I was watching, the lovers kissed each other lightly on the lips,
And strolled hand in hand to a waiting bench.
Once seated, the lovers shielded one another from the cold winds.
She whispered in his ear, he laughed (I laughed) and they kissed again.

I thought how wonderful it must be to have a special someone in your life
A special person that you could love, honor and cherish till your dying day.
Rising, as if to dance,
He took her hand in his
And they walked back to the place of their meeting.

He dropped to his knees
Like a prince to a princess
And kissed her trembling hand.
She responded with a loving hug around his neck.
As he slowly walked to catch the bus, he winked at me
Aware that I was watching all the time.
I blushed.
She remained in that same spot
Feeling the sensation of his kiss
And I went to class.

Have I told You Lately that I love you?

A good looking man is a great thing to have
You know the kind I'm talking about
Slick hair, pretty skin and a dimple on the side
That used to be the only kind of man I looked at

Then here comes Mr. Dee. He was short, bald and had a great big ole stomach
He would move from side to side when he walked and had a big grin on his face

But this man could sing like a bird and play
any instrument
He knew just what to say and how to say it.
Be glad to be alive.
He showed me how to be light and airy.
Love life, love fun, love happiness
We grew to love each other.
We were soul mates, kindred spirits
We understood each other without words.
We felt each other without fear.

"Have I told you lately that I love you?,"
He'd often say and I'd always respond "Yes,
Dee everyday."

He comforted me,
Held me, embraced me
protected me, rewarded me
demonstrated love to me
His love was void of appearance
strong, selfless, breathless, fearless,
boundless
unquenchable, yet serene

When I said things I shouldn't, acted like I
shouldn't
Ate too much, drank too much
Talked too much, too loud, too soft, too often
When I hurt him to the core, he loved me

We danced together
We laughed together

Played together
Prayed together
Cried together
Stayed together
We shared our lives together, he loved me

And when I was diagnosed with cancer,
wondered if I was gonna live or die
Spoiled, burned, wounded and bald, he
loved me
We held on to each other.
Our lives depended on it.

"Have I told you lately that I love you?"
he'd say and I said, "Yes Dee, everyday."

His kidneys failed, they had to take his toes
but they couldn't take his spirit, his drive,
his soul.
We could have grown old together,
celebrating life, anticipating tomorrow,
But God saw fit to lead him home.
He's now in that heavenly band
Singin' in that blissful choir
He fulfilled his mission in life
He was my buddy, my confidante, my
companion, my friend.
Well done, thy good and faithful servant

And now God says to him, "Have I told you
lately that I love you?", and I'm certain that
he responds, "Yes God, everyday."

Arrogance

He that dares to love and yet
refuses to become vulnerable
or needful of their lover
merely pretends
and contributes to the prophecy
of his own demise

Colors

Love the African
The Anglo
The Jew
But most of all
Gotta love you

Untitled

You strike me
The same way the sun
Strikes her rays across the ocean
The way the ocean strikes back at the shore
the way lightening strikes across the
summery sky
bold, and certain of her every move.

Oh, do be like the sunset and
The summer midnight breeze-
They never forget to return.

Untitled

Yesterday I was beautiful
Today I am even more beautiful
But not as beautiful as
I will be tomorrow
Beauty Begins Inside
Until it Spills Over
Outside

And when the rest of the world
Denies the beauty
Of my
Black skin, wide hips, nappy hair and
Thick lips
I will know that it's just
Another
White lie.

You Thought of Me

People don't have to think about me
Of the infinite amount of choices of thoughts to
think about in a day
I don't have to be one of them

So I don't take it for granted when one thinks of
me
Sends some flowers,
a card,
calls or pays me a visit
I'm honored to be one of those infinite thoughts
What a blessing that
Cannot be bought

John 3:16

For he sent down his golden son
To cleanse the earth with his blood
But people won't remember that day
They just shake their heads
And turn away.

For he sent down his only son
To bear the sins for everyone
But no one ever really cares
That they were saved
By a soul ascended from air.

For he sent down his glorious son
To make the world a better one
But as hours go by and the days linger on
God mocks this human race with scorn.

An answer to this riddle of rhyme
Is to look at man from time to time
To see if he is worthy wise
From up in the heavens
Of God's eyes.

Dear Daughter One

Don't let hopelessness beat ya
Don't let life defeat ya
Don't be afraid to try
Don't be afraid to cry
But do be afraid not to live

As seasons must change
Things can't always be the same
Sometimes hellos become good-byes
But don't forget the twinkle of the stars in
the skies

Don't always know when to let go
Can't always tell the fast from the slow
But love yourself – No matter what goes
down
Always be left with your feet on the ground

As new doors open, old doors close
Do you suppose
It's just how life was meant to be
Don't be afraid to live
Don't be afraid to give
The only guarantee that will always see you
through
Is you...

Dear Daughter Two

Don't seek fame
Don't seek fortune
Seek to do your best

Dear Daughter Three

Friends may come
Friends may go
Best friends may come
Best friends may go
Boyfriends may come
Boyfriends may go
Husbands may come
Husbands may go
But
Mother is forever

Dear Daughter Four

Remember
Being in love
Is not a license
To be
Stupid

(Untitled)

When you feel like the road
Is laden with obstacles.
Don't give up!

When you feel like you haven't
A friend in the world.
Don't despair!

When you feel like your existence
Is a big "so what!"
Don't cry!

When you feel like life
Has cheated you.
Don't worry!

Because you are not
The only one
Who is troubled.

Love

Children, love is
Getting up on a summer's morning and
watching the sun come up
Sitting in the window at night and peering at
the glistening moon
Going to the forest and seeing the animals at
work and play

Children, love is
Your mother and father telling you a bed-
time story
Your sister and brother saying their prayers
together
With you in the middle
Grandma and Grandpa coming to visit at
Christmas

Children, love is
Sitting on the front steps eating water ice
Playing tag with the kids in your neighbor-
hood
Going to school and getting an "A" on your
report

Children, love is you
Love is we
Love is the universe

Black Child

Black child, why are you crying?
We are a beautiful people
With beautiful faces
And bodies
And thoughts

Black child, stand tall
Be proud of your blackness
Show it in your walk
And in your language

Black child, you are our future
Be strong
Let your blackness
Take you far

Rope

Jump, Rachel, jump
Twist and turn.
Hop, Rachel, hop
Count one to ten.
Up and down, Rachel
Then up again.
Close your eyes Rachel
Will you win?
Jumping rope is easy
From sunup to sundown
Terry needs someone with whom to play
When Rachel's not around.

Rags

My pal Rags is not as big as I.
He's a brown ball of fur with a twinkle in his eyes.
He has a chubby little face and four brown paws.
He runs to me when he hears my call.

When I'm angry or sad, Rags comes around,
Licking my face up and down.
I love little Rags and he's the best friend ever.
He'll always be mine and we'll always be together.

Khadijah

Khadijah, only four and your grandmother's pride and joy.
You romp around the house playing with your Barbie dolls.
Dressing up in grandmother's clothes.
With a sly smile on your face
And a twinkle in your eyes.
Everyone wonders if you are an angel in disguise.

Khadijah, everyone loves you
And most of all
I do
Because you can lift the spirits
Of anyone
When they are down and blue

A Daddy Hoped For

Mailed another letter weeks ago
Ain't got no answer yet
Don't matter how many I have to send
Daddy will answer, that much I bet

Daddy, I missed you at my dance recital
I cried last night 'cause you didn't put me to
bed
Needed you to stand up for me when that
boy pulled my hair
Miss your tender tap on my head

Ain't no food in the house and everybody 's
hungry
Mama been working so hard just to make
ends meet
We don't have pretty clothes or a good
working car
How far can a few pennies stretch?
Not so far

Daddy, please write back
Come see what the matter is
You'd never leave me, you promised
I need you!
It's you I really miss
Please give me a kiss.

Momma's Here

It was the summer of "66"
I was six years old and so full of mischief
I had been in the process of keeping myself
busy while Momma was ironing.

I sneaked away, outdoors to the next-door
neighbor's backyard.
First I watched through the rusty silver gate,
the other kids playing.
Then, without asking Momma, I joined in
the game.
I was tagged it and I searched for the other
kids and found them,
But on the other side of that dreadful rusty
gate.

I started to climb, although I knew I was
headed for trouble.
The gate seemed like a huge spider web
sucking in my entire body,
But I continued to climb.

Almost at the top, it seemed like the Empire
State Building.
The ground beneath seemed like it was
sinking.

Getting ready to fly like a bird from atop the gate,
I heard a tear, then I felt a tug at my hip.
I was hung on the gate by my underpants.
Hearing the sounds of laughter and snickering from all those who saw.
Hearing people say, "That's what happens to little girls who disobey their parents."
Was it so wrong to want to play hot/cold butterbean with the other kids?
Was it so wrong to want to chase other kids with the belt and make them it?
Was it wrong for a little girl to have fun?

Momma came running to see why that crowd was laughing and pointing at her baby.
Seeing her child caught on the gate like a pinned animal was too much to bear.
Momma pushed through the crowd "Hush baby, don't cry now, Momma's here."
Released from bondage, I ran like a wounded animal, all the way home.

When night fell, I drifted off to sleep and the escapades of that day haunted me.
I heard the taunts and jeers of my playmates, their voices roaring like wild animals.
"You think you're so smart, that's why you got caught on the gate."
"Momma, Momma they're teasing me, tell them to stop."

Momma rushed to my bedside and held me
tenderly in her arms,
Daring any harm to come my way.
Echoes of my childhood keep coming back
to me.

July 1967

Here I sit on cracked cement steps winding a
piece of string around my finger
A ribbon in my plaited hair and a beau at my
side.
My white dress as pure as the first snow fits
snugly on my chubby body.
On my street, a black car is parked on the
curb,
And the ice cream truck is slowly making its
way pass my house.
In the background, a worn out screen door
opens
A white shoe approaches
Signaling dinnertime.

April (A Dedication)

It's hard to see my little sister,
Almost as grown as I.
She walks around with hand on hip,

And eyes a sparkling brown.
She tells me she's getting old,
But she's only 12.

It's hard to understand that one-day,
April will be gone to live away from the family
And start a life on her own.

It's hard to see that children won't remain
Children forever
But as long as this earth keeps revolving
And the sun spins around
April and I will always be two sisters in love

It Wasn't Supposed to Happen, But it Did

It wasn't supposed to happen, but it did
About eight years old, sittin round lookin cute
A little short skooter set on with little shapely fat thighs
and pretty legs hangin out
sittin there swingin my legs
And singin that song…"My mother told me,
if I were goodie,
That she would buy me, a rubber dollie…"

Here come Allen from cross the street
He had good looks and money to beat

He sat down beside me and talked nice and
sweet
Told me he had sump'n for me
Don't look now and don't cheat
Started rubbin gainst my legs and whisperin'
it's OK
I didn't feel good, but didn't know what to
do
He kept breathin hard like he's gonna faint
And rubbin, rubbin me, kissin' me
and pushin my head to his pants
Then I said stop, you hurtin me
He said, "give you two quarters"... here it
comes
It was big and black and look like it was
swollen with pus
"Just lick it, it'll feel better, just lick it", he
said

When he was finished and waisted his pants
We didn't know that the curtain was open
and my sister sees it all
"Ah, I'ma tell Mommy", she yclled
Allen moved so fast, I thought he had wings
stead of feet
We decided to keep it a secret, but instead
Allen blurted it to everybody, he was good
and fed
All the neighbors said I was a bad girl
wouldn't let me play with their children

My sister said. "it's time to let Mommy
know what you been doin"

Mommy and Pop was more than furious
with me
They was mad and embarrassed that
everybody knew, but them
Their child had sold herself for fifty cents,
what was the matter?
Everybody knew that I loved money so I
was blamed for everything
It was the summer vacation and I was
punished in my room
Not to go outside just to look up in that
window

"We got to do sump'n else", Mommy said,
"my child is no prostitute"
Pop was my stepdaddy, he was allowed to
beat me that day
Lay cross the bed, naked, not a stitch, today
you'll pay
All you's could hear for blocks was a
crackin of that old belt
Then a whisk of all those switches I picked
and all that hollerin, hollerin

Took me all that summer to heal from the
pain
Those whelps on my legs
turned blue and then red
Little did I know that I'd have to suffer from
a new pain
Deep down in my heart, broken and touched
I can remember that summer when I was
eight and loookin cute

Singin that old song… then someone told
her, if kissed the soldier,
Now she won't buy me, a rubber dollie
I was punished and imprisoned
Beaten, ostracized and abandoned
And I got fifty cents
Allen laid down beside me
It wasn't supposed to happen, but it did

Time

Time is something
Lovers find when there is none
Not because they
Have to,

But because they want to…

Heaven

Tell me mother, what is Heaven?
Is Heaven all fluffy and pink
Like cotton candy at a carnival
Is Heaven all glitter and gold
Like ornaments on a Christmas tree
Is Heaven all shiny and white

Like the first snow of winter
Is Heaven cloudy and dark
Like a closed closet
Is Heaven the place I shall go
When my time has ended on earth below
Tell me mother, what is Heaven?

Home Sweet Home

I'm tired and starved
Don't know who to turn to
My money's late
The rent is due
My electricity is off
My refrigerator's empty
My heart is heavy
Because no one cares
If I live or how I live
But I'll get over it
I always have before.

Pride

Can't see it…
Can't touch it…
Can't buy it…
Can't sell it…
Can't wrap it up…
Can't take it to bed…
Can't hold it or talk to it…
Then why do you die for it?

I'm Different

Was always different from other children
Thick pointy glasses and eyeballs that
wouldn't stop moving
Much as I tried to see clear and very far
Squinted and frowning' nothing helped
I just couldn't, just couldn't
Still I learned to ride a bike, play double
Dutch and hopscotch
Couldn't play no kind of ball
Was sorry as sorry could be
Yet I knew I was smart, smarter than most
Could spell like a bee, do math with a buzz
and read on a wing
Life's funny like that, I suppose

As I got older, I was more ashamed of what
I couldn't see
Didn't want others to know, tried to hide it
whenever I could
Wore contacts and pretended to see when I
really didn't

Even drove a car for a while, thank God I
gave it up when I should
Gotta be like everybody else, gotta be
normal when I can
That's the way, I felt, can't help it, that's me
Today I'm older and wiser to boot
I know it OK; everybody is different in
some way

Now it's called a disability and not a
handicap
You can do everything that other people do,
just in a different way
Put my thick glasses back on
Read real close up
Ask for help when I can't see the sign
Cause now I'm still bright, smart and
intelligent
Things I have always been
But now I know, it's OK
I'm, simply, different, that's all

Pursuit

I see him now, behind that tree with the
scribling"Mary loves John."
He is dressed in a beautiful brown suede
coat.
The tips of his black leather shoes glisten in
the sun and I am caught.
I duck behind a bench until he passes.
And the smell of his cologne (Pierre Cardin,
I think) sends a tingling,
Sensation throughout my body.
His footsteps are mine and soon I will be at
his front door.
I will be able to see how the man of my
dreams lives.
Outside his window, I peek in.
I find another woman.

Could she be a sister or a neighbor from
across the way?
I take in a little more of the scene.
He kisses this stranger gently and I am hurt.
How could he do this to me?
Can't he see that I'm the only one for him?
I stagger from the window, like an animal
wounded in battle.
Cupid has shot his last arrow through my
heart.

On the bus, I press my nose against the cold
window pane.
Tears trickle down my face, and I am re-
minded of many loves lost.

He Told Me What I Wanted to Hear

Here he comes
A new man
He's different from all the others
I know he's the one

He loves me and I love him
Buys me flowers and dines me
Tells me I'm beautiful, funny and smart
I willingly gave him all my heart

Gradually things began to change
It was so gradual, I didn't notice
My friends didn't come around anymore
No one called ... He had control of my life

If I turned to the right or I turned to the left
I had to always answer to him
First a push, then a slap, a hard hit and
finally a full-fledged fist-fight
He told me that no one else would ever love
me like he did

What started out like a dream ended up like
a nightmare
He told me what I wanted to hear
There's something deep down inside of me
I can't make it rest
It is lonely and scared and has a great fear

I got out of that situation
God's angels protected me
Can't ever let that happen again
He told me what I wanted to hear

The Heart of a Mirror

I stood in the mirror and examined myself
Got paid yesterday and went out and got my
hair did, yeah
I went to Sax last night and got me this real
pretty dress
Honey, it's made out of silk, not that polly
stuff I usually wear
Let me make sure the tags are still on
Lord don't let me get nothing on it 'cause

I got to take it back tomorrow
Look at my shoes, look good on my legs
Nobody would ever know they were stalleno knockoffs
I know that I'm looking good today

Somehow as I went out that day, that mirror kept looking back at me
That image seemed to keep callin my name, but I didn't recognize it
I tried to answer, but my mouth had no sound
I could only listen to that little tiny voice keep callin my name
But I couldn't recognize it

I carried on with my day and enjoyed the attention I got
Everybody looked at me with envy
They thought I had it all
Then I happened to notice a little lady sitting off to the side
She was dressed in sloppy clothes and appeared to be needy
Before I could get over to offer her some help
A man offered her his hand and took her to her car
She got in a long white limousine and rolled up the window
I ran behind and yelled, hey wait! Can I get a ride?

Dresses long, dresses short, hair long, hair short
Wavy hair, kinky hair, braided hair, weaved hair
Light skinned, dark skinned, tall and short
Thin nose, big nose, full lips,
Muscular, petite, skinny, fat, whatever, whatever
We all want to fit a mold, a pattern, an acceptance, a standard

Who makes the standard and at what cost do we conform

"Man looks on the outside, but God looks on the inside
"Where a man's heart is, so is he'
The colorless, the uniqueness
That special part of us
I stood there. The mirror came back
Right in my face
Now I understood
I suddenly recognize my new name
It was, the heart, the heart, the heart

From the Heart of a Fat Lady

Used to be five foot three inches tall and two hundred ponds
Now I'm pushing towards one forty and lovin the ride

Life now is so different; I'll have to tell you
about it
What used to be and now is and I'm taking it
in stride

Used to wobble from side to side when
walking
My shoes would quickly run over no matter
what kind they were
Had to wear queen size pantyhose in all
those ugly colors
We can't talk about the sound that fat thighs
make when they rub together

Used to shop in big lady stores where they
had clothes in only three colors
I tried on clothes to see what fit not what
looked the best on me

Shoes had to be in a wide size, dresses had
to be in tent size

There was not too much cute for me

In the summer, I wore long skirts or pants to
hide those big knees
Couldn't wear sleeveless tops for the same
reason…hide those arms
When I sat down I tried not to let the double
rolls of my stomach show
I never seemed to know where to fold my
arms, over it or below

But the worst part of being fat is not the fat
nor its discomfort
It's the stares and the disgust and the shame
from others you get
People thought all that I did was eat...they
didn't know I starved a lot
They didn't know my sorrow, my pain, my
fears or how angry I got

People say, just stop eating, just lose it, just
lose it
They will never know how hard it is, it just
ain't that easy
Going up and down the scale
Being frustrated and queasy

Today I stand on the other side of the crystal
ball
I shop in any store, wear what I want and fit
any kind of shoe
People no longer stare, but ask me what
would I like to eat
It's amazing how quickly people forget that
I used to be fat

Life now is wonderful, I'm happy and
thinner
People now accept me as a winner
I'm still the same person
Hope next time you see a fat lady that you
think of me
Being fat ain't no joke and that's a fact

My Christmas Evolution

Was a little bitty baby, bout six months
Everybody was 'cited cause it was
Christmas time and I was home
Spent all that time in the hospital in an
incubator
Was born only three pounds
Couldn't see too good, so they sit me right
in front of that big Christmas tree
It was people and presents and decorations
all over the place
All I see's is those bright pretty lights
Mama gave me some cake and I smudged it
all over my face
That was a good Christmas

Well I grew up a little bit, getting bigger
everyday
Was about five years old and it was
Christmas Eve and I didn't want Santa
To catch me up
Sat by my bed sayin my prayers
Now I lay me down to sleep, I pray to the
Lord my soul to keep...
And Santa can I please have that baby doll
and a game set and a ball and jump rope and
a slide and and and a and a---
Mama yelled in my room, "girl cut that light
out and go to bed"

That was a good Christmas
Time waited 'round for nobody
I imagine by now I was about ten years old
I had been in my bed for hours and heard my parents downstairs
I quietly sneaked down the stairs to see what was happenin'
Those stairs kept squeakin
I kept stopping and a startin
They had just finished decoratin the tree and putting up the gifts
Daddy was sittin there letting Mama feed him that cake I made for St Nick.
"Honey, I tell you that is some nasty cake"
"You know she tries, you got to eat it for her sake"
I got so excited, I sprang from around the corner
"I knew it was no Santa Claus, I knew it! I knew it it!"
"Girl, what are you doing up?", Mama said in a loud voice
I forgot I was supposed to be in bed, oops that was my choice

And that was a good Christmas
Now I'm a teenager, what a time that was
Mamma said all the family was comin over for Christmas dinner
So we had to be on our best behavior
Last year I had to pretend I liked all those ugly gifts

Aunt Mary bought me a poka dot dress with lace at the bottom
And Uncle Charlie bought me a biker's cap
What am I gonna do with that
I'm a a teenager now tryin to do my own thing
Just show me the money- the money- the money...
That is all I could sing
And that was a good Christmas

I've been in college now for about two years
Got all my stuff packed up cause I'm goin home for Christmas
I'm so smart and proud of myself
I'm getting educated and can speak well
Going to show those folks at home I got a new life and a new way
All that Christmas stuff is the white man's way of doing things
I now celebrate Kwanza, Words like Nia are now in my head
What a difference that Christmas was

Haven't had one like that since
I can say without a doubt that was a good Christmas
Went on to get married
Had a little baby of my own
We watched her grow from toddler to teen
Pampers, clothes, toys, sports and boys
Every Christmas was different, yet all were the same

I always prayed the same prayer
Now I lay me down to sleep, I pray to the
Lord my money to keep
Yet I cherish each one for I say to you again
They all were good Christmases'

Now I'm sitting here thinking about
Christmas coming up again
Children all gone, but grandkids are now
here
Gotta make sure that they have lessons in
piano, dance, karate and the like
Want to make sure that they are cultured,
secure and very polite
Grandchildren are joys
That second chance God gives you to
correct your mistakes
This Christmas will be a good Christmas
like all the others
For goodness sakes
I plan to live a long life
Around ninety-two I suspect
By then I imagine I won't hear good nor be
able to see
They'll sit me down right in front of that
pretty Christmas tree one day
People and decorations will cover the place
And all I'll see are those big pretty lights
And somebody will give me a slice of some
good ole cake
I'll just eat it and smudge it all over my face
But that too will be a good Christmas

Crystal Ball

I felt the smack on my bare, brown bottom
Welcoming me into this strange and new world
I saw the bright white lights of the operating room
Glaring into my tiny unfocused eyes
I felt the warmth of lying close to my mother's breast
I tasted the sweet milk of her love
I heard babies cry around me and I joined in
I touched myself here and there because
I was a person, singular, apart from
My mother's womb
I felt my mother's hands,
So soft, so careful
Changing me
Coddling me
Loving me
I felt my father holding me in his strong arms and
I heard him thank God for a healthy daughter
I tasted all the varieties of Gerber's baby food
And I was satisfied
I felt my grandparents holding me close to their hearts

I heard the praises and congratulations to my parents

From everyone who saw this precious human being
Who would one day be able to sit down and write
About this moment-the joy of birth
I saw the season change from spring to fall
The leaves change from orange to yellow
And the sky from blue to gray
I grew up into an inquisitive 6 year old
I felt proud because my parents
Were in the audience of my kindergarten
School play, cheering me on as I strutted
Across stage in my red and white soldier's uniform
I heard a joyful cry from the lips of my parents
When my baby sister was born
I cried too, because now I had someone to care about
To caress and to love other than my doll baby
I was saddened when we had to part
Her destination—army
I smelled hot buttered oatmeal
Coming from the kitchen of
My first home
I saw the season change from fall to winter
The barren trees left alone in silence

I saw people dressed in black, crying
Because
My grandmother who had cared for me
As a small child, was gone forever

I felt the sorrow of Martin Luther King's
death
I saw uncertainty on the faces of my people
I saw faces of pain and resentment
I saw faces of agony and bitterness
I saw faces of hate and of pride
I saw Malcolm X, Marcus Garvey, and I was
them
I saw myself black and beautiful and proud
to be
I fantasized a world of peace, but our leaders
were gone
I saw the years go by
I felt proud to be a part
of the new generation-college students
I saw the Cathedral of Learning with its tall
spires
Leaning against the sky
The oblong shaped School of Law with its
Maze of classrooms
The castle like School of Dental Medicine
And I decided that I would go as far
As my intellect
Would take me
I felt the harshness of professor's grades
Grading me on what they thought was....
That mighty pen, poised and ready
To "F" up my life
Then I realized that the only obstacle before
me
Was myself
I saw the season change from winter to
spring

I saw the frost melt from every petal of
every flower
I heard a newborn baby's muffled cry, thank
God
For the breath of life
I smelled fresh air around me
And I was moved to sprout
Wings like a bluebird and
Fly, fly, fly
I felt wanted by my main squeeze
When he said
He loved me
And pain
When we had to part
I saw my cousin's eyes in a dream
She didn't require any assistance
Because she was immortal
I felt pain because I would never be able
To see my cousin again,
Except in dreams
I felt pain because Debbie died at 19
From barbiturates and alcohol
I saw the Philadelphia 76 er's lose the
basketball championship 5 times
And Muhammad Ali win the boxing
championship 3 times
I heard police sirens screeching on a hot,
sticky day
Guns being fired from all directions
And in the end
An old man lay bleeding in the gutter
Because he was in the wrong place at the
wrong time

Police say it was an accident, but a human life was gone
I saw the season change from spring to summer
The grass became green
The flowers turned pink, yellow and red
I dreamt
I was in Africa
I was dressed in beautiful African silks and called Queen
I saw life all around me
The beauty and wonder of it warmed my soul
I touched the hand of a blind man to show him

Somebody gave a damn about him
I saw a nuclear war and the earth I loved destroyed
I saw faceless and legless bodies strewn everywhere
I became an immortal being and I saw a new kind of people
Who could live on forever,
Never having pain or suffering
I saw paradise and my mother and father beckoned
Me to join them in this new world
I saw the past, present and future of my life
And I cried
A pool of unreflected tears
Because I had lived

Nikki

I will feel you
When the wind is blowing
I will see you
When the snow is falling
I will hear you
When the leaves are scattered
I will hold
Your smile and everything that mattered
In the dearest possible place...
In my heart.

Sdia

I lie alone in a bed that is not mine
In a room that belongs to someone else
So quiet, so perfect, so clean
Men and women in spotless white clothes
wrestle to care for me
My mind is scattered
My body is weak
My spirit is broken

The fat from my bones has escaped me
The mirror portrays a face I don't recognize
Frowned, frayed, wrinkled and discouraged
Sores plague my body inside and out
Blisters sprinkle my hands and feet
Each part of my body is wracked by pain
People are frightened by me

One moment of indiscretion
One short minute of pleasure
One miniature second when I did not protect myself
I put my life in the hands of someone else
In the name of "love"
I was betrayed
This has become my destiny

Mom

Mom passed over to be with the Lord when I was only seventeen
So long ago, yet her impact upon my life was as if it were yesterday
Though I am grown and have a child of my own
I hear my voice speak her words to my child

I watch my feet walk in the places she used to visit
I feel my hands touch in the way she used to touch

I can barely remember her voice or remember the things she used to wear
I can't even find the place where she used to work or the restaurant she used to frequent
Yet her spirit continues to strive with me
Her love constantly abides with me

Her encouraging words of wisdom continue
to speak to my heart
It's just as if we have not been apart

I thank God for the woman my mother was
So strong, so spontaneous, so independent
I am the person I am today because of the
seventeen years she gave me
Though I wished there had been more
I am thankful that God lets her live on in my
soul

Debbie (1959 – 1979)

I can remember when we were children
And our mothers used to push us
In twin strollers.
You were always bigger than I
And how we used to fight.
Who would have thought that I
Would one day go to college?
And you would stay at home.
We made a pact and vowed
To never separate
But…We were children then.
Do you recall when you received
Your first doll.
You didn't want to share her
And I cried and cried
Because I thought that you were mean.
But when I gave you my ice cream

You let me play...
But not for long.
As we grew up
We went our separate paths
Because you were so different
From I.
But we kept in touch
Because after all
We still were first cousins.

When you needed my help
I was there
And when I needed you
You knew.

I have tried many times
To understand the reason why
We'll never laugh or talk again
Why we'll never share secrets
Why we'll never ever be
Happy again...
That same way when
We were children.
But ... as everyday goes by
And every hour
I'll never forget
My dear cousin
Because I loved her so.

Lord

May the earthly things
That don't matter
Not be confused today
With the things that really do

God Is

God is the strength of my life
Without him, I have no purpose
I have no destiny,
I have no peace

When family fails
When friends are no longer there
Sometimes there is no money
Other times there is no food
When I need a lawyer
And even when the doctor's have given up
God is

A long time ago God made a way
For everyone to know that he loves us
I'm so glad he did
For without him, I would fail
Like a ship without a sail
Yes it is true without any doubt
God is

Mary Magdalene

Speak sweet Jesus; you are with us once again.
The tomb which encased your being has been rolled away.
Oh, how long I have waited to kiss your loving feet
Oh, how long I have waited to have you place your loving hands upon my head
Rejoice sweet Jesus, the feast has been prepared
The feast of roasted duck, kneaded bread, red wine, fruit and fish is waiting
To be given your holy blessing.
Everyone is waiting to celebrate your homecoming
Speak sweet Jesus; you are with us once again.

A Change of Rules

Sitting around playing and joking with my daughter
She has big breasts and I didn't
That was her claim to fame
I cupped my left hand under my left breast and said
"this is how a breast should look"
Suddenly my joke turned serious and then there was fear

I felt a lump about a size of an orange
That for me was clear

Talked to my partner
We needed to agree
Better go to the doctor
Don't worry about the fee
Mammogram, second mammogram
Flatten down, oh what pain
Ultrasound, consultation, biopsy
Just a benign tumor
I have everything to gain
To my surprise, the doctor spoke a different tune
You have breast cancer and it's late
We have to operate

Gave me a bunch of pamphlets
I wiped my tears and fled
Me and my partner just held on to each other
that being said
They took the breast and made another out
of my stomach
You never would have known
Today I have a flat tummy
Had to go through extensive chemotherapy
That was the worst part
It took away my hair, made me sterile and
weakened my bones
Intense radiation was to follow
I screamed on the inside I felt so hollow
Just when I thought it was all over

"You Got to take the other breast?", I
screamed!
The doctor said I was at a high risk for
reoccurrence

Prevention is the key!
Today I live with a different set of rules
Have to wear wigs, tattooed eyebrows and
acrylic nails
Used to define myself by my outward ap-
pearance
Spent many hours and lots of money to
make it so

After feeling ugly, unattractive and
sometimes lonely
Plenty of secret pity parties and times of
insecurity

After much prayer and introspection
Without breasts, hair,nails,and those things I
can't mention
I now know that I am more than outward
appearance
I stand now with boldness and strength
Knowing that God chose to preserve me
It's what's on the inside that counts
For that,I have plenty of courage

I am my Momma's Child

Strong, proud Black Woman
From whom
The Oak Tree gets its strength
Rooted in the belief
in the Almighty
lived an Almighty life;
and left behind a legacy so
rich
that all of the lives raised with
The touch of her hand
must follow it-

"Treat Everybody right!";
so simple, yet so profound
Nations would rise up and
Be at Peace
If only they had her wisdom…

Biography

Dr. Portia Yvonne Bookhart

Portia Yvonne Bookhart is the oldest child in a family of six. Her parents are Robert Bookhart and Yvonne Bookhart. She is from Philadelphia, Pennsylvania and is a proud graduate of Overbrook High School. From there, she went on to receive a Bachelor of Arts degree in English Writing from the University of Pittsburgh, a Master of Arts degree in Administration and Supervision from the University of the District of Columbia and a doctorate in Curriculum and Instruction from Virginia Tech. Her Doctoral dissertation, "Perceptions of Learning-Disabled Students, Their Teachers, and Support Staff" shared information on a child's life in the special education program.

She has taught in DC Public Schools for 20 years, English to sophomore students who marvel at her intellect and wit. She has been a Cafritz Scholar and her proposal, "Combating Writing Anxiety Using the Journalistic Approach" afforded her the opportunity to explore the teaching of journalism.

Through her use of poetry, she is able to express the message that there is a light at the end of the tunnel, and that success is there for anyone who wants it. They just have to work at it.

Dianne Alynda Carson

Dianne Alynda Carson is the middle child of Robert Butler Carson and Ruth Carson Bishop. Although she has spent most of her life in the DC area, her roots are from South Florida. She is the proud mother of one daughter and one beautiful grandbaby. She received a Bachelor of Science degree in Mathematics and Philosophy from Howard University and two Masters degrees from the University of the District of Columbia in Family Counseling and Mathematics Education. Additionally, she has several hours of graduate studies towards a Doctorate in Mathematics Education at the American University.

For the past twenty-five years, she has taught mathematics to students at Cardozo and Ballou Senior High Schools in Washington, DC. For some of that time, she taught in Shrewsbury, England and Frankfurt, Germany. She has been privileged to be the recipient of several prestigious awards such as the McDonald's Teacher of the Year Award and holds the titles of Fulbright and Cafritz Scholar.

Though much of her career has been in the thrust of mathematics education and the teaching of theories, recently, she discovered the art of telling stories via poetry and dramatic presenttions. She says mathematics affords her the philosophical and logical orientation to express critically and argumentatively a variety of experiences

in her own personal life. Though these experiences are often viewed as dramatic and sometimes tragic, these life changing events have made her a stronger and more courageous individual.
She desires to talk abut the "unspoken and hurtful" parts of life. Although they are not the most desirable topics to share with everyone, they can not be avoided. She says that they walk and talk with us and sometimes haunt us when we are unaware.
She hopes that her poems will inspire, encourage and uplift the wounded and disheartened. Those that lack hope will discover hope and those that are in need of deliverance will find it. Additionally, those that are whole might believe that they may remain so regardless of circumstances and despite the present reality.

Sierra Leone Joyce

Sierra Leone Joyce was born in Washington, D.C. She is the proud mother of Tifanne Elizabeth Lawrence and Leander Chantelle Lawrence.
Ms. Joyce is a graduate of Bennett College and George Washington University receiving her certificate in Paralegal Studies in 1993. She is also published in Who's Who of American Teachers 2004-2005. While she has taught English for two years at Ballou Senior High School, Washington, D.C., she is embarking on her 13th year as an educator.
She currently teaches English at Crossland High School in Prince George's County.
Ms. Joyce is a published poet and also enjoys writing short stories. She is in the process of her fifth book of poetry.
Ms. Joyce attributes all of her success to God and her late parents: Louis and Helen Joyce.

About the Editor

The editor is a son of an immigrant. He holds a B.A. M.A.T and Doctoral degrees. His life has been devoted to education issues, social issues, political issues, and a deep concern for the environment. His experiences include:

- Former Special Assistant to the Associate Superintendent of the District of Columbia Public Schools

- Elected to the Democratic State Committee for two four-year terms

- Published and has written a dozen articles and books

Two publications that received top critical reviews are:

"What Students Consider a Good Teacher"

"Does a Teacher's Personality Influence Learning"

- Taught in preschool, elementary school, middle school, (junior high school), senior high school and college

- Former Assistant Principal in the District of Columbia Public Schools

- Has written numerous proposals and conducted workshops

- Holds Divisional Superintendent License for the State of Virginia

The editor is currently preparing a publication on *The American Educational Dilemma: High Stakes Cheating and High Stakes Testing.*

His latest publication is *The Buying and Selling of Education in America.* Amazon. Com rated the book four out of a possible five stars.